En

"In this age of chaos simplicity is a gift. Jennifer Waddell has laid out a simple refreshing 21-day guide to praise. Praise is powerful, creating a God-portal. It along with faith, prayer and the Word are foundational to breakthrough. Jennifer has captured this revelational understanding and releases the power of praise. It takes 21 days to create a habit. She's challenging us to do just that. Praise changes things. Thanks, Jennifer!"

Barbara J. Yoder
Lead Apostle, Shekinah
Regional Apostolic Center
Ann Arbor, MI

"Jennifer Waddell's book, *21 Days of Praise*, is therapy for the spirit, mind and emotions! The reader starts the day with a powerful time of thankfulness to the Lord. Waddell helps the person develop their own personal spiritual spa as gratitude to the Lord fills the atmosphere. She encourages the person to journal their song, praise and prayer for the day. Reading through this book every 21 days will break a person out of discouragement and into a life filled with the joy of the Lord!"

Barbara Wentroble
President, International Breakthrough Ministries and
Breakthrough Business Leaders
Denton, TX

"This inspirational writing on praise is an encouragement and elevation for the body of Christ today. Jennifer's heart of wisdom shines."

Henry Adams Jr., Pastor
Believer's Christian Center
San Antonio, Texas

"There is something about praise —the fruit of our lips released as a love song for The LORD that shifts the atmosphere around us, beckoning heaven to manifest tangibly on earth. Each day, for the next 21 days, Holy Spirit and Psalmist Jennifer Waddell invite you to journey with them into the very Heart of God. One song, one moment of praise, one prayer at a time. The reward of His Presence awaits you! Step into the overflow...you will never be the same!"

Dr. Bernardine Wormley Daniels
Soterios Ministries, Inc. & Strength to Strength, LLC
Dearborn Heights, MI

"21 Days of Praise is a much needed devotional for the days in which we live. Jennifer, a true lover of Jesus, has done an excellent job of reminding us to look up and not allow our focus to be on anything other than giving God praise at all times. Each day, and oftentimes multiple times within each day, we should direct our attention towards the truth that our Father is a good, good God. Jennifer has done an excellent job in sharing her joy of praise and worship with every reader. The world is filled with so much that invades our thoughts day in and day out. This devotional gives us a tool in which to direct our thoughts towards a heart of praise, worship and thanksgiving. It is life giving, easy to read and God focused. It works with a morning cup of coffee, a break at the office, a quiet time of prayer, or a simple reminder before sleep. Make sure you give one to a friend in need. I am looking forward to volume two. Congratulations, Jennifer, on taking this step of faith!"

Tonya Roberson, Apostle
Tonya Roberson Ministries
Berkley, Michigan

"Now is the time for the Body of Christ to ascend on the wings of worship and prayer. We will only ever go as high as we pray and worship, otherwise we are grounded. You hold in your hands a flight manual. Time to go up! Enjoy the ride."

Benjamin Deitrick
Pastor, Shekinah
Regional Apostolic Center
Ann Arbor, MI

"A must read! I love how Jennifer has put together beautiful truths from scripture in a simple devotional format that will take you higher in praise and deeper in worship. Whether you are looking to go deeper in your personal life or in a corporate setting, these scriptural truths will help take you higher places in praise and closer to the Father's heart in worship."

Steve Hansen
Kingdom Ministries International
Southfield, MI

21 Days of Praise

21 days to look up and refocus through praise

Jennifer Waddell

Cover design by Steve Hansen

ISBN-13: 978-0-692-17679-5
Printed in the United States of America

DEDICATION

I dedicate this book to my wonderful husband, William, who would give me the world if he could, my amazing children, Terence, Terri, and Tina, who are all such a joy and my gifts from God, to all of my beautiful grandchildren that the Lord has blessed me with, and to my great-grandson who puts a smile on everyone's face. Most importantly, I dedicate this book to my loving heavenly Father who has blessed me so richly, beyond my wildest dreams. Thank you.

Table of Contents

The Bible says that God is holy. Today we praise Him because He is holy, meaning that He is separate, and set apart from man. He is without fault, pure, righteous, and sacred. He is the One who is worthy of praise. We praise Him because of who He is, not just for all of the great and wonderful things He has done. The Bible also says that His ways are higher than ours. He is mighty, powerful, full of grace and mercy, and His love endures forever. Those are good reasons to lift up His name, give Him praise, and bless Him today.

"Exalt the Lord our God, and worship at His footstool – He is holy." Psalm 99:5 (NKJV)

ACKNOWLEDGMENTS

A huge thank you to Shelley Ozment, without whose help I would still be saying, "I'm going to write a book one of these days". Thank you to Barbara J. Yoder for seeing the gift of writing in me and allowing me to contribute to the writing of her book, *Taking on Goliath*. Thank you to Barbara Wentroble for all of the encouragement and prayers that helped me through some very difficult times over the years.

To my sister, Janie E. Bibbie, for her "fine tooth comb" editing, Julie Smith-Spears for her valuable input, and to Steve Hansen for the great cover, thank you. And to all of those who have faithfully prayed, and loved me, and believed in me over the years, you know who you are (too many to list here), thank you.

Introduction

What would happen if we began and ended everyday with praise? What if upon arising in the morning and before going to bed at night we said, "Thank you, Lord, for this day, and for your goodness and your great love!" instead of some of the other things that we say that don't give God praise.

We should see a notable difference in our lives if every day we filled the atmosphere with praise. The Bible says that the Lord inhabits the praises of His people. The Lord comes and fills the room as we begin to give Him praise. Praise changes the atmosphere. As we praise, the atmosphere around us changes from one of despair and dread to one of peace and hopefulness. All of our enemies leave the room at the sound of praise to our God. Also, there is a change in our attitude as we change our altitude.

Instead of concentrating and thinking on things that weigh us down, we should, as the Word of God says, "Think on these things, the things that are lovely, honest, just, pure, virtuous, and praiseworthy". We will then begin to see things from heaven's perspective and we are able to rise up above the cares of this life.

What is praise? It is extolling the Lord with our voices, declaring His goodness and His greatness, magnifying Him, for who He is, what He has done, and what He will do. Praise is an act of faith. Even when we can't see things changing around us for the better, we still believe that God will do what He said He will do and so we thank Him before we see it. And no matter what we see or don't see, what is happening or is not happening, we still say that God is good. That is praise.

Come with me on a 21-day journey of praise and let's see what happens. Let's begin and end each day with a song of praise, scriptures that exalt the Lord, and testimonies of His goodness. I have left room for you at the end of every day, to write your song, your praise, and your prayer. I believe that our lives and our situations will surely change as a result of the time that we spend in His presence praising His name.

"I will bless the Lord at all times. His praise will continually be in my mouth." Psalm 34:1

Day 1

Look Up and Refocus

I will bless the Lord at all times,

His praise will always be in my mouth.

I'll give thanks to the Lord for He is good,

His praise will always be in my mouth.

As we begin our 21 days of praise, we look up and focus our attention on the Lord. Hebrews 12:2 says, "Looking unto Jesus, the author and finisher of our faith..." We give Him praise for His love, His mercy, and His goodness. God inhabits the praises of His people. As we praise the Lord, He comes and begins to fill our lives and we can see His wonderful works and His goodness to us. In Psalm 116:12, the question is asked, "What shall I render unto the Lord for all His benefits toward me?" The answer that we will give today is that, "I will offer the sacrifice of thanksgiving... Psalm 116:3a" and I will praise the Lord!

"Bless the Lord, O my soul: and all that is within me, bless His holy name." Psalm 103:1 (KJV)

My Song:

My Praise:

My Prayer:

Day 2

Praise for Who He Is

Holy, holy, holy! Lord God Almighty!
Early in the morning our song shall rise to Thee;
Holy, holy, holy, merciful and mighty!
God in three persons, blessed Trinity!

Holy, holy, holy! All the saints adore Thee,
Casting down their golden crowns around the glassy sea
Cherubim and seraphim falling down before Thee,
Who wert, and art, and evermore shall be.

Holy, holy, holy! Tho' the darkness hide Thee,
Tho' the eye of sinful man Thy glory may not see;
Only Thou art holy; there is none beside Thee,
Perfect in power, in love, and purity.

Holy, holy, holy! Lord God Almighty!
All thy works shall praise Thy name, in earth, and sky, and sea
Holy, holy, holy; merciful and mighty!
God in three persons, blessed Trinity!

John Bacchus Dykes, Reginald Heber
Public Domain

The Bible says that God is holy. Today we praise Him because He is holy, meaning that He is separate, and set apart from man. He is without fault, pure, righteous, and sacred. He is the One who is worthy of praise. We praise Him because of who He is, not just for all of the great and wonderful things He has done. The Bible also says that His ways are higher than ours. He is mighty, powerful, full of grace and mercy, and His love endures forever. Those are good reasons to lift up His name, give Him praise, and bless Him today.

"Exalt the Lord our God, and worship at His footstool – He is holy." Psalm 99:5 (NKJV)

My Song:

My Praise:

My Prayer:

Day 3

Praise for His Goodness

Praise the Lord, for He is good,
And His mercy is forever.
Praise the Lord for He is good,
And His mercy is forever.

Oh, that we would give Him praise,
Oh, that we would bless His name,
Oh, that we would give Him praise,
For His mercy is forever.

For the Lord is good,
The Lord is good,
And His mercy is forever.
Yes, the Lord is good,
The Lord is good,
And His mercy is forever.

Psalm 107:1 tells us to give thanks to the Lord for He is good. As we continue to read through this chapter, we are reminded of the things that God did for the children of Israel, how He delivered them from their enemies, out of their distresses, out of darkness, healed them, and brought them to their desired haven. We need to remember from time to time, the good things that God has done for us. Has He delivered you from your enemies? Has He brought you out of your distress? Has He healed you? Has He given you air to breathe? Has He given you food to eat? Has He given you clothing? Oh, that we would praise the Lord for His goodness to us!

"Oh, that men would praise the Lord for His goodness, and for His wonderful works to the children of men!" Psalm 107:8 (KJV)

My Song:

My Praise:

My Prayer:

Day 4

Praise for His Faithfulness

Faithful you have been,
And faithful you will be,
You are always near, and Lord,
You always hear me.

I will lift up my prayer to you,
And I will praise your name.
You answer when I call,
You are faithful.

Today, We can call on the Lord and make our request known to Him. He is always listening, always near, and ready to come and help us. He is our salvation and our high tower. We can run to Him and be saved. He is faithful to keep us, to lead us and guide us throughout this day and every day. We praise the Lord for His faithfulness, His lovingkindness and His tender mercy.

"For the Lord is good and His mercy is everlasting..." Psalm 100:5 (KJV)

My Song:

My Praise:

My Prayer:

Day 5

Praise for All That He Has Made

Praise to the Lord, the Almighty
The King of creation
O my soul, praise Him
For He is thy health and salvation
All ye who hear, now to His temple draw near
Praise Him in glad adoration

Praise to the Lord Who o'er all things so wonderfully reigneth
Shelters thee under His wings
Yea, so gladly sustaineth
Hast thou not seen how thy desires e'er have been, Granted in what He ordaineth

Praise to the Lord
Who doth prosper thy work and defend thee
Surely His goodness and mercy here daily attend thee
Ponder anew what the Almighty can do
If with His love He befriend thee

Praise to the Lord, O let all that is in me adore Him
All that hath life and breath
Come now with praises before Him
Let the 'amen' sound from His people again
Gladly for aye we adore Him

Public Domain

When we look out over the beauty of God's creation, we can't help but praise Him. There is something about nature, the water, the earth, and the sky, that fills us with awe and wonder. Today, let's take time to look at the wonderful creation of God, even if only in a picture, and give Him thanks for all that He has done. Whether it is Spring, Summer, Fall, or Winter, there is beauty in every season. Thank you, Lord, for the beauty of your creation!

"He has made everything beautiful in its time..." Eccles. 3:11 (KJV)

My Song:

My Praise:

My Prayer:

Day 6

Praise the King of kings and Lord of lords

Your name is Holy,

Yes, your name is Holy.

You are high and lifted up and you reign in victory.

You are seated on the throne and

Your train fills the temple.

You reign in majesty, in majesty,

and you deserve all of the glory.

Your name is Holy,

Yes, your name is holy.

You are high and lifted up and you reign in victory!

Jesus Christ is King of kings and the Lord of lords. Let us see Him high above all of our circumstances and allow Him to rule and reign in every area of our lives. Today, let us praise Him and exalt Him in our hearts. Is there some area of your life that you haven't yet submitted to His lordship? Now is a good time to surrender and to give the control over to Him. He is well able to take care of and to perfect all that concerns you and me.

"Be still and know that I am God; I will be exalted among the nations, I will be exalted in the earth!" Psalm 46:10 (NIV)

My Song:

My Praise:

My Prayer:

Day 7

Praise for His Blessings

Oh, how great is your name!

You are greatly to be praised!

In the city of our God, in the holy place,

You are greatly to be praised!

You are worthy of honor and blessing

You are greatly to be praised!

Your greatness is unsearchable,

You are greatly to be praised!

Oh, how great is your name!

You are greatly to be praised!

How can we begin to count all of the blessings that we have received from the Lord? His blessings to us are more than we can number. Let's begin today by counting the ones that we know that He has done for us this day alone. As we remember the things that He has done for us, we are no doubt overwhelmed by His goodness!

"Great is the Lord, and greatly to be praised, in the city of our God, in the mountain of His holiness..." Psalm 48:1-2 (KJV)

My Song:

My Praise:

My Prayer:

Day 8

Praise His Great Name

The name of the Lord is a strong, strong tower,

The righteous run to Him and they are saved.

Yes, the name of the Lord is a strong, strong tower,

Let the righteous run to Him and be saved.

For there is no other name but the name of Yeshua,

There is no other name but the Lord.

There is no other name but the name of Yeshua,

There is no other name but the Lord.

Today, praise the Lord for His powerful name, that name that is above every other name. As we praise His name, the atmosphere around us changes. Even just the whisper of His name causes peace to come and to settle down around us as well as in us. Praise His name today and see the salvation of the Lord.

"The name of the Lord is a strong tower. The righteous run to it and they are saved." Proverbs 18:10 (NKJV)

My Song:

My Praise:

My Prayer:

Day 9

Praise for His Holy Spirit

Peace, peace, wonderful peace,
Coming down from the Father above!
Sweep over my spirit forever, I pray
In fathomless billows of love!

Warren D. Cornell and W. George Cooper
Public Domain

Today, praise the Lord for His Holy Spirit who is always with us and who is our Helper. The Holy Spirit is here to help us to walk in the Spirit, and not after the flesh. Today, we can mind the things of the Spirit as He directs us.

Ephesians 5:18 tells us to be filled with the Spirit. As we are filled with the Spirit we are enabled to walk in the Spirit, keep our mind stayed on Him, and stay in perfect peace. May today be a day filled with perfect peace as you begin the day with praise.

"You will keep in perfect and constant peace the one whose mind is steadfast [that is, committed and focused on You—in both inclination and character],
Because he trusts and takes refuge in You [with hope and confident expectation]."

Isaiah 26:3 (Amplified)

My Song:

My Praise:

My Prayer:

Day 10

Praise for His Continual Presence

We come into your presence,
We lift our thoughts above.
We've set our hearts to seek you,
To know you and your love.

We kneel here in your presence
And unto you we sing.
We bless you Lord,
We praise you, God,
Forever, Lord, and King.

We stand here in your presence,
We lift our hands and say,
We love you, Lord,
We give you, Lord,
You're worthy of the praise.

Today, praise the Lord for His continual presence. He is always with us. Praise the Lord today because He is with you, whether you are in the darkest of nights or in the brightest daylight. You may be in a situation right now where there seems to be no way out or you could be having the time of your life. God is with us even in the darkest night and will bring us through. There was never a night that did not end, nor a cloudy day that did not eventually pass and the sun break through. Remember that He has said, "I will never leave you nor forsake you." (Heb. 13:5 KJV) Praise the Lord!

"...I will never leave you nor forsake you."

Hebrews 13:5 (NKJV)

My Song:

My Praise:

My Prayer:

Day 11

Praise the Creator of All Things

All things bright and beautiful,

All creatures great and small,

All things wise and wonderful,

The Lord God made them all.

Praise the Lord who created all things. All of the beauty that we see around us in nature, in the sky above, and in the earth below, has been created by God. We also are His workmanship. Ephesians 2:10 says that "we are His workmanship, created in Christ Jesus unto good works..." (KJV). We were created by Him and for Him. Praise God today as the Creator of all things, to whom belongs all of the praise, the glory, and the honor.

"For by Him were all things created, that are in heaven, and in earth, visible and invisible, whether they be thrones, or dominions, or principalities, or powers: all things were created by Him and for Him."
Colossians 1:16 (KJV)

My Song:

My Praise:

My Prayer:

Day 12

Praise and Thanksgiving in His Presence

The righteous will give thanks to your name,

They will forever live in your presence.

They will give thanks to you and bless your name,

For you are worthy of praise and honor,

You are worthy of praise and honor.

As we stand, or sit in the presence of the Lord, and quiet ourselves for a moment and begin to think about His goodness to us, we can't help but praise Him. There is something about being in the presence of the Lord that causes joy to rise up within us, and just a spirit of gratitude and thankfulness. We offer Him our thanks as we quiet ourselves in His presence today. Thank you, Lord.

"Surely the righteous shall give thanks unto thy name: the upright shall dwell in thy presence." Psalm 140:13 (KJV)

My Song:

My Praise:

My Prayer:

Day 13

Praise As An Offering to the Lord

We bring you an offering of praise,

We come before you with hands upraised.

We are so thankful to you,

And we bless your name.

We bring you the sacrifice of praise.

We bring you an offering of praise,

We come before you with hands upraised.

We give to you willingly,

We give because you gave,

We give you our offering of praise.

Praise is the offering that we want to bring to the Lord today and every day. The children of Israel were told to bring an offering so that the house of the Lord, the Tabernacle, could be built. God desires to have a dwelling place among His people today but it is a place that is not made with hands. We are His tabernacle, His dwelling place, as we offer up praise to Him. The Bible says that He inhabits or is enthroned on the praises of His people. Let us build Him a place with our praise. Today, we bring our offering of praise to the Lord so that He can come and live in us.

"Speak unto the children of Israel, that they bring me an offering: of every man that giveth it willingly with his heart ye shall take my offering." Exodus 25:2 (KJV)

My Song:

My Praise:

My Prayer:

Day 14

Praise for Ears to Hear And A Voice to Praise Him

We praise you, Lord,
for ears that hear
What your Spirit is saying.
We praise you, Lord,
because you hear us,
Whenever we are praying.

We praise you, Lord,
because your Word is true.
We praise you, Lord,
for making us brand new.

We praise you, Lord,
for teaching us your way.
We praise you, Lord
for another glorious day.
We praise you, Lord
for another glorious day.

Have you ever stopped to think about what a blessing it is to be able to hear, or to speak, or to see? Or someone may be reading this book to you because you are not able to read it yourself. Did you ever stop to think what a blessing it is to have someone that will read to you? Today we praise the Lord because He hears us whether we speak out loud or even if we can't speak at all. He hears us whenever we pray. Why don't we let Him hear our voice today in a song, a prayer, and in our praise and thankfulness to Him for giving us another day to offer Him our praise.

"My voice You shall hear in the morning, O LORD: In the morning I will direct it to You, And I will look up" Psalm 5:3 (NKJV)

My Song:

My Praise:

My Prayer:

Day 15

Praise the Lord for This Day

This is the day that the Lord has made

And I will rejoice and be glad.

This is the day that the Lord has made

And I will rejoice and be glad.

Be glad, be glad!

I will rejoice and be glad!

Be glad, be glad!

I will rejoice and be glad!

For the Lord is good,

The Lord is good.

For the Lord is good and worthy to be praised.

For the Lord is good,

The Lord is good.

For the Lord is good and worthy to be praised.

This is the day, whether cloudy and gray, or as sunny as a day in May,
Whether birds perch and sing or take to their wings,
Whether we walk or run, cry or have fun,
This is the day that was made for us to enjoy,
Every man, every woman, every girl, and every boy.
So, lift up your voice, and sing to our King,
Our God, our Lord, who made everything.
For this is the day that He has made,
Rejoice and be glad, for He is worthy of praise.

"This is the day which the Lord has made: we will rejoice and be glad in it.
Psalm 118:24 (KJV)

My Song:

My Praise:

My Prayer:

Day 16

Praise Him for His Provision

Today I will give Him thanks.
Today I will keep my mind on Him.
Today I will put my trust in Him.
Today I will praise Him.

Today I will call upon His name.
Today I will keep my eyes on Him.
Today I will be filled with His Spirit.
Today I will praise Him.

Today, I will listen to His voice.
Today I will not be afraid.
Today I know that He will guide me.
Today, I will praise Him.

There are many things in this life that call for our attention. Our thoughts may go to the work that lies before us for the day, getting the children ready for school, or we may just not be feeling well in our bodies this morning. But before we start with the busy-ness of the day, thinking about all that surrounds us here in this natural realm, let us stop and praise the Lord, putting Him first.

Matthew 6:33 says "But seek first the kingdom of God and His righteousness and all these things shall be added to you." What things? Well, what do you need today? Food, clothing and shelter are normally at the top of the list. So, before I get my breakfast, and before I decide what it is that I will wear today, let me take a moment to thank the Lord for another day and for the fact that I have something to eat and I have something to wear, and I have a roof over my head. Thank and praise the Lord today for His provision. He is our Provider and for that, we give Him praise.

"But seek first the kingdom of God and His righteousness and all these things shall be added to you." Matthew 6:33 (NKJV)

My Song:

My Praise:

My Prayer:

Day 17

Praise Him for He is My Rock

Lord, you are wonderful,

Lord, you are marvelous,

Lord you are faithful,

Faithful and true,

Lord, we love you.

Lord you are glorious,

Lord you are victorious,

Lord you are worthy,

Worthy are you,

Lord we love you.

Let the fragrance of our worship

fill this room.

Today, stop for a moment and consider that the Lord is our Rock. He is the same, yesterday, today and forever. He never changes and can be depended on to always be there, always watching, leading and guiding us. He is our strong tower and we can run to Him and be saved from all of our enemies.

"The Lord is my Rock, and my fortress and my deliverer, my God, my strength, in whom I will trust..." Psalm 18:2 (KJV)

My Song:

My Praise:

My Prayer:

Day 18

Praise the Lord With Singing

Sing to the Lord a new song,
Sing to the Lord all the earth.
Sing of His salvation,
Sing to Him all the earth.

Sing about His goodness,
Sing about His love,
Sing about His mercy,
Sing to Him all day long.

Sing about His power,
Sing about His grace,
Sing of His lovingkindness,
Sing of Him in every place.

For the Lord is great and greatly to be praised,
Sing and bless His name.
For He is mighty in power and matchless is His name,
Sing and bless His name.

We don’t always feel like singing first thing in the morning. Some of us need that cup of coffee to get us going. Some of us just wake up slowly and are not quite awake first thing in the morning. This is day number 18 of our 21 days of praise so maybe we are beginning to start a new habit of arising early in the morning and giving God praise. Only three more days to go and this early morning praise will be a part of our morning routine. Today let us tell ourselves, I will praise the Lord, and then let’s do it!

"Oh, sing to the LORD a new song! Sing to the LORD, all the earth. Sing to the LORD, bless His name; Proclaim the good news of His salvation from day to day. Declare His glory among the nations, His wonders among all peoples."

Psalm 96:1-3 (NKJV)

My Song:

My Praise:

My Prayer:

Day 19

Praise the Lord for His Watchfulness

This is my Father's world,

and to my listening ears

all nature sings, and round me rings

the music of the spheres.

This is my Father's world:

I rest me in the thought

of rocks and trees, of skies and seas;

his hand the wonders wrought.

Maltbie D. Babcock, 1901

Praise the Lord that He never sleeps or slumbers. Even when we are sound asleep, He is watching over us, our family and friends, our cities, and our nations. Praise the Lord that He never forgets about us, whatever it is we are going through, whatever issues there are surrounding us and those that we care about, whatever challenges that we are facing locally, nationally, and internationally, God cares and is working all things together for good for those that love Him and are called according to His purpose. As we praise Him today, we remember that He is always watching, and is ever mindful of us.

"He will not allow your foot to be moved; He who keeps you will not slumber."

Psalm 121:3-5 (NKJV)

My Song:

My Praise:

My Prayer:

Day 20

Praise the Lord for the Overflow

Fill us with your love,
Fill us with your Spirit.
Let us love like Jesus loves.
Fill us with your life.

Let us overflow with your love.
Let us overflow with your Spirit.
Let us overflow with your life.
Fill us till we overflow.

As we praise you,
Let us overflow.
As we adore you,
Let us overflow.
Fill us with your presence, Lord,
Let us overflow.

It is impossible for us to pour out our praise on the Lord and He not pour back His blessings on us. He doesn't bless us because we praise Him but He blesses us because He is good. There is a great reward in lifting up our praises to the Lord in our words and in our songs. There will come a time when there is an overflow. Today, we want to continue to fill the atmosphere with our praise and see the overflow that will come as a result.

"There is a river whose streams shall make glad the city of God, The holy place of the tabernacle of the Most High. God is in the midst of her, she shall not be moved; God shall help her, just at the break of dawn." Psalm 46:4-5 (NKJV)

My Song:

My Praise:

My Prayer:

Day 21

Praise Him Because He is Worthy

O, Come let us adore Him,
O, Come let us adore Him,
O, Come let us adore Him,
Christ the Lord.

For He alone is worthy,
For He alone is worthy,
For He alone is worthy,
Christ the Lord.

Finally, on this last day of our 21 days of praise, we want to praise the Lord just because He is worthy of praise. We read in Revelation where the angels are crying out, "Worthy is the Lamb who was slain, to receive power and riches and wisdom, and strength and honor and glory and blessing!" (Rev. 5:12). For all of the reasons that we have to praise the Lord, this is the highest and greatest of them all. We praise Him because He is worthy to be praised. He created us to give Him praise. So today, and every day, we give Him praise if for no other reason than because He is worthy. Amen? Amen!

"Thou art worthy, O Lord, to receive glory and honor and power..."
Revelation 4:11 (KJV)

My Song:

My Praise:

My Prayer:

Praise God from whom

all blessings flow

Praise Him all creatures

here below

Praise Him above ye

heavenly hosts

Praise Father, Son, and Holy Ghost.

Amen.

Thomas Ken
Public Domain

ABOUT THE AUTHOR

Since receiving Jesus Christ as her personal Savior on Thanksgiving Day 1980, Jennifer has been on a journey to know God. Jennifer believes that God has gifted her to bring hope and encouragement to people through teaching, singing, and through her writings. Jennifer changes the atmosphere whenever and wherever she speaks or sings. Jennifer is a psalmist, songwriter, worship leader, teacher, and author whose work is sure to reach and touch the hearts and lives of many people.

Jennifer presently serves as the Praise and Worship Leader for the Ann Arbor Aglow Lighthouse which meets monthly at Washtenaw Community College in Ann Arbor, Michigan, where she was formerly employed as a Clinical Instructor for nursing students.

Jennifer has a deep love for God and for people, and a passionate desire that all would know Him, from the least to the greatest of them, and that they would all be filled with the love of God, and demonstrate that love to the world.

Jennifer lives in Ann Arbor, Michigan with her husband, William. They have three children, and have been blessed with eighteen grandchildren, and at the writing of this book, one great-grandchild.